# MIGHTY
# MACHINES

Authors: Adam Hibbert, Chris Oxlade and James Pickering

Illustrators: Stephen Angel, Peter Gregory, Colin Howard, Graham Howells,
Mike Lacey, Mike Taylor, Ross Watton (SGA)

Cartoonist: Peter Wilks (SGA)

Editor: James Pickering

Consultant: Steve Parker

This edition designed by Design Principals and Starry Dog Books.

This is a Parragon book
This edition published in 2007

Parragon
Queen Street House
4 Queen Street
Bath BA1 1HE, UK

British Library Cataloguing-in-Publication Data

A catalogue record for this book is available from the British Library.

ISBN 978-1-4054-6678-3

# MIGHTY
# MACHINES

*p*

# Contents

## CHAPTER TWO
### SHIPS

## CHAPTER THREE
### CARS

## CHAPTER FOUR
### TRAINS

## CHAPTER FIVE
### MOTORBIKES

## CHAPTER SIX
## TRUCKS

## CHAPTER SEVEN
## AIRCRAFT

## CHAPTER EIGHT
## SPACECRAFT

## CHAPTER ONE

# RACING MACHINES

# Who raced a horse and carriage in a train?

In 1825, George Stephenson raced his engine Locomotion against a team of horses, and won. For the first time ever, he showed that a mechanical vehicle could travel more quickly than a horse-drawn carriage.

Locomotion

**Amazing!** Racing machines have been around for a very long time. The Romans used to race horse-drawn chariots more than 2,000 years ago. Their chariots had two wheels which were connected by a wooden axle. It must have been a bumpy ride. The drivers used to stand up to drive, for balance. The more horses, the faster the chariot went.

## Is it true?

*In 1897, a cyclist beat a motorbike in a race.*

**YES.** A man called W.J. Stocks pedalled over 43 kilometres on his bicycle in one hour, and beat a motorbike by 270 metres. The rider of the motorbike was not happy. He said that the crowd was too noisy and had put him off!

Early motor race, France 1902

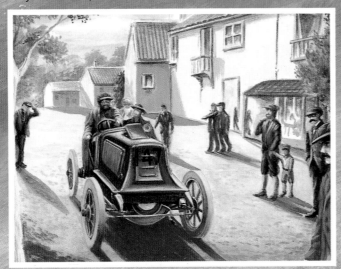

## Who first raced in cars?

The first ever race was in 1894 between Paris and Rouen in France. The Count de Dion won in a steam-powered car, which could only manage 18 kph. Early motor races showed people that cars were as fast and reliable as horses.

9

## ? Who used a rocket to go faster than 1,000 kph?

In 1970, American Gary Gabelich drove his rocket powered car, The Blue Flame, at 1,016 kph through the Bonneville Salt Flats, and it's still the world's fastest rocket car. When he wasn't breaking records, Gary also raced dragsters and worked as a test astronaut.

Thrust SSC

## ? Who put a rocket on a bike?

Richard 'Rocketman' Brown started building The Challenger in 1996. It has three rocket engines, which produce about 12,200 horsepower per tonne, taking it to 530 kph!

Challenger

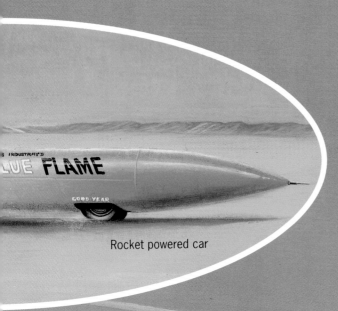

Rocket powered car

##  Is it true?
*Some cars need parachutes.*

**YES.** Some cars are so fast that brakes alone aren't powerful enough to stop them. Parachutes drag these cars back to lower speeds when they're travelling very quickly. Thrust SSC has four parachutes to bring it back below the sound barrier.

## ? Who went faster than the speed of sound in a car?
Briton Andy Green set a world record in 1997, when he drove the jet-powered Thrust SSC at 1,227.985 kph through the Nevada desert.

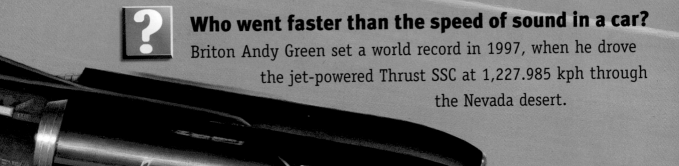

Gobron-Brillié

**Amazing!** As early as 1904, some cars could travel at more than 160 kph! Louis Rigolly was the first person to reach this speed in his enormous 100 horsepower Gobron-Brillié car, during the July Speed Trials in Ostend, Belgium. Luckily he didn't crash. Seatbelts hadn't been invented, and Rigolly only wore a cloth cap to protect his head!

Although go-carts are much smaller than other racing cars, they can reach speeds of up to 250 kph! Carting is very popular among young drivers, and many Formula One stars, like Michael Schumacher, used to race carts.

## ? Which cars race to a formula?

There are very strict formulas or rules about how racing cars are built. Formula One cars' size, shape and petrol tank are all governed by rules, so that every race is fair.

Ferrari Formula One racing cars

## Is it true?

*Modern racing cars have wings.*

**YES.** They are at the front and back of the car. A racing car's wings are carefully designed to stop the car from taking off. As air passes over the wing, it pulls the car down on to the track. This gives the driver better control and roadholding.

Indycar

## ❓ What's an Indycar?

Indycar racing takes place at the Indianapolis Motor Speedway in America. Indycars have powerful engines and huge fins.

## Which cars race for 24 hours?

❓ Sports cars race around the Le Mans circuit in France for 24 hours. Two or three drivers take turns at the wheel to drive the car as far as possible.

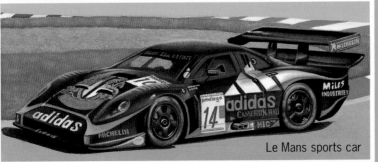

Le Mans sports car

# Who uses their knees to go round corners?

Riders in motorbike Grands Prix take corners very quickly by leaning sharply into bends, scraping their knee against the track. This is called the 'knee down' position. For protection, they have tough nylon knee pads sewn into their leathers.

Sidecar racing bikes

# Which motorbike racers have three wheels?

Sidecar racing bikes have three wheels. The sidecar isn't powered, but the second rider provides vital balance. On corners, the sidecar rider leans out, for extra roadholding, and the driver hardly has to reduce speed.

**Amazing!** Some bikes have tyres with metal spikes sticking out from them, for riding on ice. The spikes pierce the icy surface and stop the bike from skidding. Without them, both bike and rider would go flying!

*Knee down position*

**Is it true?**
*Motorbike races last only one hour.*

**NO.** Different races have different lengths. The famous Le Mans race in France, for example, lasts for an exhausting 24 hours, while speedway races are often run over just four laps (1,200 metres) and last for about a minute!

## Which motorbikes don't have brakes?

Speedway racing bikes don't have brakes. Instead, the bike slows to an almost instant halt, as soon as the throttle is released. Riders wear extra sturdy steel boots, which they grind into the dirt, to bring the bike to a final standstill.

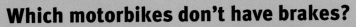

*Speedway racing bikes*

## Who races across the Sahara?

Competitors in the Paris-Dakar Rally set off from the French capital and race for 20 days, until they reach the capital of Senegal, West Africa. Cars have to withstand extremes of temperature, and the rigours of travelling through the dust and sand of the Sahara desert.

**Amazing!** In trials competitions, high speeds are not allowed! Trials riders jump over obstacles, with penalties for putting a foot on the ground. They mustn't go faster than 24 kph.

Rally carts

## What are rally carts?

Rally carts are speedy four wheeled, outdoor go-carts, designed for cross-country racing. They have wide tyres to cope with bumpy ground, powerful engines, and roll-cages, in case of a tumble!

16

## Is it true?
*Some bikes have three wheels.*

**YES.** Many ATVs (All Terrain Vehicles) have three wheels. They can be raced or used on farms for getting around safely and quickly. Quad bikes have four wheels, with thick tyres and improved suspension.

Motocross

## ? Which racecourse has jumps?

There are plenty of jumps and bumps on cross-country motorbike scrambles or motocross. Riders roar across the toughest terrain there is, through muddy woods, fields and even snow!

17

## Who wears a crash helmet at sea?

Powerboat drivers have to wear crash helmets. Powerboats are made from tough aluminium and each crew member is attached to a cord which cuts the engine if they fall out. These boats can reach 220 kph (120 knots)!

**Amazing!** Powerboats can take off. At high speed, air can become trapped beneath them, lifting the boat above the water, with disastrous results.

Powerboat

## Who's the fastest man on water?

Kenneth Warby managed an official speed of 511 kph (276 knots) in his hydroplane Spirit of Australia in 1978, on Blowering Dam in Australia.

Hydroplane

## ? Which boats use water jets?

Jet boats and jet skis use water jets to power them. In the same way that the jet engine of an aircraft forces hot gas backwards, sending the plane forwards, a water jet pushes pressurised water backwards, driving the boat forwards. Bumpy but great fun!

Jet ski

### Is it true?
*Some racing boats are powered by fans.*

**YES.** Hovercraft are powered by fan-like propellers, mounted high in the air, so they can travel over land as well as water. Underwater propellers would get clogged with weeds in swampy rivers.

## What were Gee Bees?

American Gee Bee planes raced during the 1930s. The company which made them was called Granville Brothers (G.B.). These short, fat planes used to race at speeds of nearly 480 kph, in 8,800 kilometre-long races! Plane races were run to show how reliable the aircraft were.

## What was the longest air race?

The longest air race was the MacRobertson race from Mildenhall, England, to Melbourne, Australia, in 1934. It was won by the crew of a de Havilland in a time of 70 hours and 54 minutes.

MacRobertson race

## Is it true?

*The first non-stop flight around the world was made in 1933.*

**NO.** Wiley Post did make the first solo round the world flight in Winnie Mae in 1933, but he had to stop several times to refuel. It was a 25,000 km journey, and it took him just over a week.

Winnie Mae

**Amazing!** The first non-stop around the world flight wasn't until 1986. It took Dick Rutan and Jeana Yeager nine days to make the 40,000 kilometre journey. Their lightweight aeroplane Voyager had just 68 litres of fuel left when it landed at Edwards Airforce Base.

Gee Bees

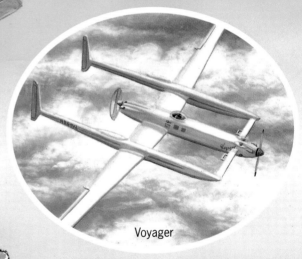

Voyager

## When was the first air race?

The first air race was in 1909, near Reims in France. It took place only six years after the very first flight by the Wright brothers.

21

# CHAPTER TWO

# SHIPS

# Who crossed the Atlantic on a bunch of reeds?

In 1970, Thor Heyerdahl, a Norwegian scientist and explorer, and his seven crew, crossed the Atlantic Ocean in a sailing boat made from reeds. The trip showed that sailors from Ancient Egypt could have made the journey in reed boats thousands of years before Christopher Columbus in 1492.

Papyrus reed boat Ra II

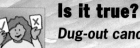

## Is it true?
*Dug-out canoes are still used today.*

**YES.** Dug-outs are still made and used in many parts of the world. They are used for fishing and paddling along rivers. Fishermen who live on islands in the Pacific, such as Tonga, sail out to sea in dug-out canoes with outriggers (small side hulls) which help the canoe to balance.

## Who hollowed out logs?

Ancient people made boats called dug-out canoes by hollowing out large tree trunks. They scraped and chipped the wood out with simple tools. Dug-out canoes were amongst the first types of boat.

Dug-out canoe

Coracle

## Who went fishing in animal skins?

Fishermen in Wales and Ireland used to go fishing in small boats called coracles or curraghs. They were made by covering a framework of bendy sticks with animal skins. A few fishermen still use canvas coracles today.

Viking longship

## Who rowed for a long time in a longship?

About 1,000 years ago, Viking warriors rowed their longships when the wind blew from the wrong direction, or stopped blowing altogether. Longships were sleek wooden ships with a single square sail, used for exploring and launching raids.

### Is it true?
*Boats can be rowed with one oar.*

**YES.** Some boats, such as gondolas in Venice, are rowed with a single oar. The rower stands at the boat's stern (back) and rows by sweeping a long oar from side to side.

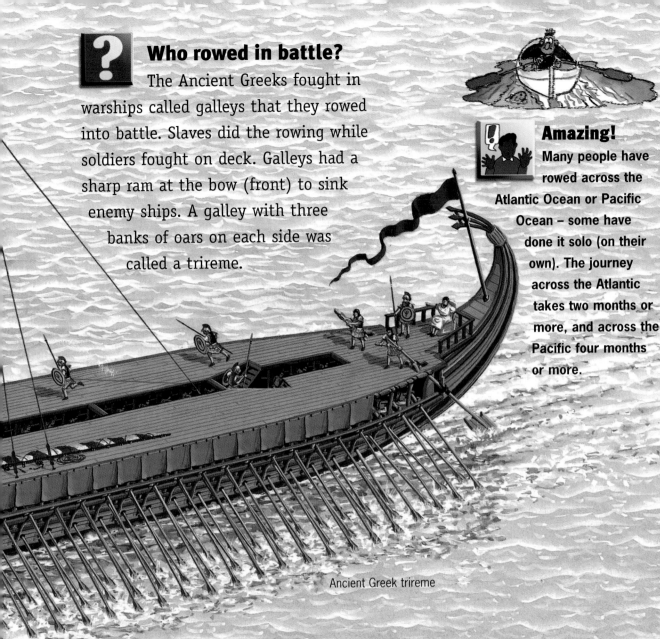

## ? Who rowed in battle?

The Ancient Greeks fought in warships called galleys that they rowed into battle. Slaves did the rowing while soldiers fought on deck. Galleys had a sharp ram at the bow (front) to sink enemy ships. A galley with three banks of oars on each side was called a trireme.

### Amazing!

Many people have rowed across the Atlantic Ocean or Pacific Ocean – some have done it solo (on their own). The journey across the Atlantic takes two months or more, and across the Pacific four months or more.

Ancient Greek trireme

Rowing eights

## ? Who steers an eight?

An 'eight' is the crew of a racing rowing boat. The ninth member, the cox, tells the rowers what pace to row at, and steers with a small rudder at the back of the boat.

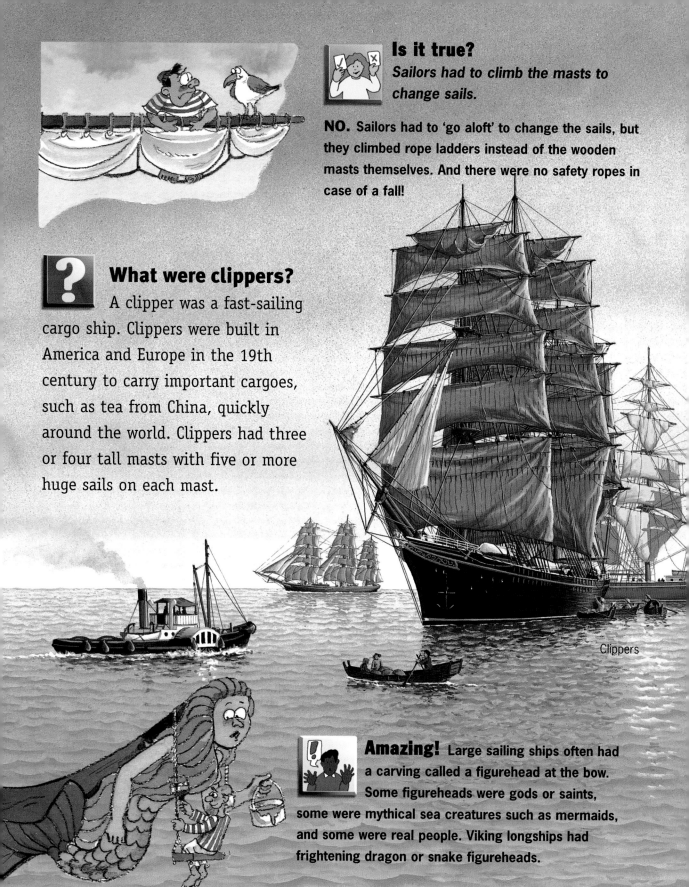

## Is it true?

*Sailors had to climb the masts to change sails.*

**NO.** Sailors had to 'go aloft' to change the sails, but they climbed rope ladders instead of the wooden masts themselves. And there were no safety ropes in case of a fall!

## What were clippers?

A clipper was a fast-sailing cargo ship. Clippers were built in America and Europe in the 19th century to carry important cargoes, such as tea from China, quickly around the world. Clippers had three or four tall masts with five or more huge sails on each mast.

Clippers

**Amazing!** Large sailing ships often had a carving called a figurehead at the bow. Some figureheads were gods or saints, some were mythical sea creatures such as mermaids, and some were real people. Viking longships had frightening dragon or snake figureheads.

Mayflower

## What was a galleon?

Galleons were trading and fighting ships used in the 15th and 16th centuries. The galleon Mayflower took the first pilgrims to America in 1620.

## Who went to sea on a junk?

Chinese sailors have been going to sea in ships called junks for more than a thousand years. Junks have cloth sails strengthened with bamboo poles. Large junks have five masts. Junks were the first ships to have a rudder to help them steer.

Chinese junk

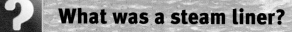

## What was a steam liner?

A steam liner was a steam-powered passenger or cargo ship that crossed oceans on set routes at set times. In the 19th and 20th centuries, millions of people emigrated from Europe to America on steam liners, taking their own food and bedding.

### Is it true?

*Anchors are used to slow ships down.*

**NO.** Anchors stop ships from floating away with the wind or tide. Anchors catch in rocks or sand on the seabed.

**Amazing!** Modern cruise liners are like huge floating hotels. There are cabins for thousands of passengers, restaurants, cinemas, theatres and lots of swimming pools.

## Which modern liner has sails?

The luxury cruise liner Club Med has sails as well as an engine. Using the sails when the wind blows saves fuel for the engine.

Club Med 1

RMS Queen Mary (launched 1934)

Tug

## ? **What does a tug do?**

A tug is a boat with very powerful engines that pulls or pushes large ships. Tugs help to move ships in and out of port. They also go to the rescue of broken-down ships, and tow them back to port to be repaired.

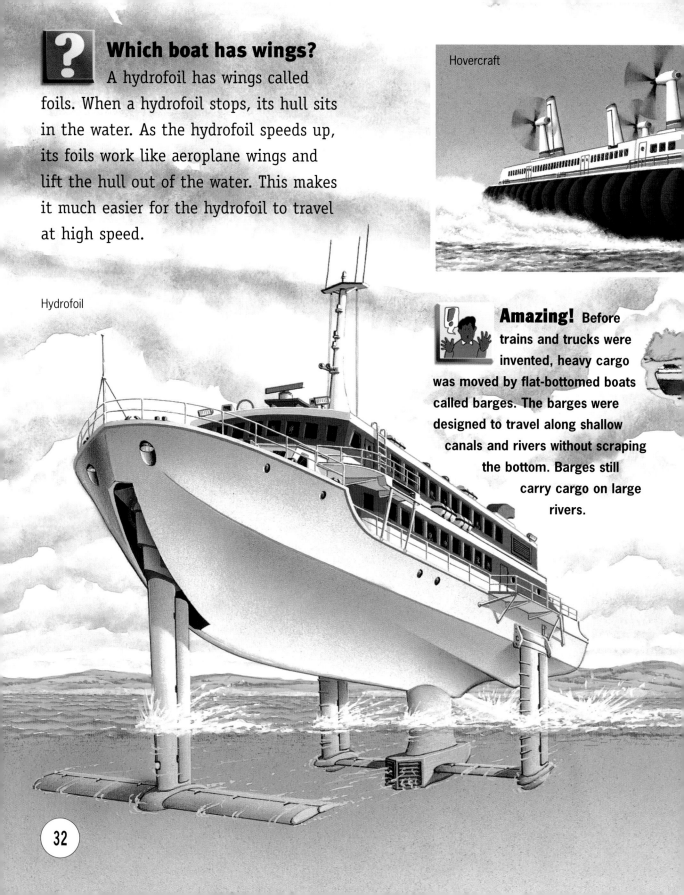

### ? **Which boat has wings?**

A hydrofoil has wings called foils. When a hydrofoil stops, its hull sits in the water. As the hydrofoil speeds up, its foils work like aeroplane wings and lift the hull out of the water. This makes it much easier for the hydrofoil to travel at high speed.

Hovercraft

Hydrofoil

**Amazing!** Before trains and trucks were invented, heavy cargo was moved by flat-bottomed boats called barges. The barges were designed to travel along shallow canals and rivers without scraping the bottom. Barges still carry cargo on large rivers.

## Which boat flies?

A hovercraft is a boat which skims just above the water on a cushion of air. Huge fans blow air under the hovercraft. A rubber skirt holds the air in place. The hovercraft is moved along by propellers.

## Which ship has two hulls?

A ship or boat with two hulls is called a catamaran. Catamarans can travel more quickly than ships with one hull which are called monohulls. High-speed ferries such as the SeaCat are catamarans. They have a top speed of more than 40 knots.

### Is it true?
*Some ships have three hulls.*

**YES.** A ship with three hulls is called a trimaran. Most trimarans are sailing yachts. They have a large hull in the centre and two small side hulls. When one small hull is in the water, the other is in the air.

SeaCat

# Which ship is a floating airfield?

An aircraft carrier has a huge, empty flat deck where aircraft take off and land. The aircraft take off from the bow using a catapult. They land again from the stern. Hooks on the planes catch a wire on deck, and stop the planes with a jolt. Underneath the deck are hangars where the aircraft are stored and serviced.

American aircraft carrier

**Amazing!**
The first gun battle between two ironclads (warships with iron armour) took place in 1862 during the American Civil War. The Monitor and the Merrimack fired at each other but no great damage was done.

## ❓ What was a pocket battleship?

Pocket battleships were small, fast, German ships in the 1930s. Only three of them were built. Each had six huge guns, armour more than 60 millimetres thick and powerful diesel engines.

Admiral Graf Spee pocket battleship

### Is it true?
*Some ships are nuclear-powered.*

**YES.** Some large submarines, some aircraft carriers and some ice breakers have nuclear-powered engines. They can travel for several months without having to refuel.

## ❓ Which ship is invisible?

The United States Navy 'stealth' warship doesn't show up clearly on enemy radar. Like the stealth aircraft, its special shape and paint scatter enemy radar signals making it very difficult to detect.

Stealth warship

## Is it true?

*Most ships are jet powered.*

**NO.** Most ships have diesel engines that turn their propellers. But some ships, such as high-speed ferries and warships, have turbines that work like aircraft jet engines.

Powerboats

## ? What is a yacht?

The word yacht normally means a sailing boat with a cabin below, or set into, the deck. People use yachts for cruising and for racing. The crew of a yacht has to 'set' (adjust) the sails to make the best use of the wind.

A small sailing boat without a cabin is called a dinghy.

Yachts

## Which boats can travel the fastest?

The fastest boats are powerboats, with top speeds of about 120 knots (220 kph). Most powerboats are used for racing. They have huge outboard engines at the back and skim across the water's surface, bouncing against the waves and any trapped air beneath them.

**Amazing!** Some boats are pushed along by water jets. A powerful pump sucks in water from under the boat and squirts it out of the back. This shoots the boat forwards. Jet-skis also use water jets.

JANNINE 31

25

Surfer

## Who surfs across waves?

Surfers ride down the sloping faces of waves balanced on their boards. Expert surfers can stay on a wave all the way to shore. They often ride through the 'tube' formed by the curling top of the wave.

37

## How big are submarines?

The biggest submarines are nuclear-powered naval submarines. The biggest of all are Russian Typhoon submarines. They're 171 metres long (as long as two football pitches) and weigh 26,500 tonnes. They can stay under water for months on end and sail around the world without refuelling.

World War Two U-boat

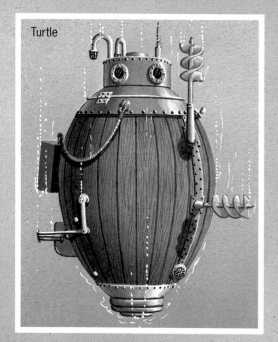

Turtle

**Amazing!** The first working submarine looked like a wooden barrel. It was built in 1776 and was called Turtle. The operator sat inside and pedalled to make its propellers turn. Turtle was designed to attack ships by diving under them and fixing a bomb to their hulls. But it was never successful.

## What was a U-boat?

U-boats were German submarines used in World War One and World War Two. U-boat is short for underwater boat. U-boats sank thousands of ships. They crept up silently, hidden under the water, and fired missiles called torpedoes. The torpedoes zoomed through the water and exploded when they hit the ships.

## Is it true?

*Submarines use sound to see.*

**YES.** A submarine's sonar machine makes beeps of sound that spread out through the water. If the sound hits an object in the water, it bounces back to the submarine and is picked up by the sonar machine. The machine works out how big the object is and how far away it is.

Operating the periscope

## What is a periscope?

Submarine crews use their periscopes to see ships on the surface above them when submarines are submerged. The top of the periscope sticks just above the surface. It works using several lenses and prisms (triangular pieces of glass).

# CHAPTER THREE

# CARS

## What was a horseless carriage?

A horseless carriage was a horse-drawn carriage with an engine in place of the horse. The first horseless carriages were powered by steam. In England by the 1830s some passenger services were operated with steam coaches. But the coaches were slow, noisy and dirty, and wrecked the cart tracks!

Daimler and his first car

James's steam carriage 1829

## Who invented the first car?

Two German engineers, Karl Benz and Gottlieb Daimler, both built working cars in 1885. Each car had a small petrol engine to drive it.

**Amazing!** When mechanical vehicles first appeared in Britain, a man had to walk in front of them carrying a red warning flag (or a red light at night). The Red Flag Law was introduced because other road users, such as horse riders, complained about the danger.

## Is it true?
*The first cars didn't have steering wheels.*

**YES.** The steering wheel did not appear on cars until the late 1890s. Before that, drivers steered with a lever, like the tiller on a boat, or by spinning handles on a small upright wheel on the end of a vertical pole.

## ? Which was the first car to be sold?

The first car to be sold was a three-wheel model built by Karl Benz. The first owner was a French engineer called Emile Roger, who bought his car in 1887. Soon Benz had a factory building cars for sale, but only a few of the three-wheelers were sold.

Benz Patent-Motorwagen

## ? Who drove a Silver Ghost?

The Silver Ghost was one of the first cars built by the Rolls-Royce company. Only rich people could afford to buy one, and they normally employed a chauffeur to drive it! Like all Rolls-Royce cars, the Silver Ghost was famous for being very quiet and extremely well made.

Austin Seven

## ? Which car was very cheap to run?

The Austin Seven was so economical that it used half a penny's worth of petrol to travel a kilometre. The Seven was so tiny that it was often called a 'toy' car, but it was very cheap to buy.

## Is it true?
*Taxis have always had meters.*

**YES.** The word taxi is short for taximeter cab. A taximeter was a meter designed in 1891 that recorded the distance that a horse-drawn cab had travelled. When engine-powered taxis were introduced in 1907, they also had to have a meter.

# Who went on trips in a charabanc?

Factory workers and their families used to go on days out to the seaside or to the city in a vehicle called a charabanc. A charabanc was like a wagon with benches in the back for passengers to sit on. The first charabancs were pulled by teams of horses.

Rolls-Royce Silver Ghost

Bugatti Royale

**Amazing!** The Bugatti Type 41 Royale was designed by Ettore Bugatti to be the most luxurious car ever. His idea was that every royal family in Europe would buy one. The car was 6.7 metres long and had a 12-litre engine. But only six Royales were ever built, and only three were ever sold. Today, if a Bugatti Royale ever appears at auction, it fetches millions of pounds.

## What was the 'Tin Goose'?

'Tin Goose' was the nickname of a short-lived rear-engined car called the Tucker '48. It had many original features, such as a strong passenger safety compartment and a third headlight which swivelled as the driver turned the steering wheel.

Tucker's Tin Goose

Citroën Traction Avant

## Why was the Citroën 7CV so special?

The Citroën 7CV of 1934 was the first popular car driven by its front wheels. It was known as the Traction Avant. It was also one of the first cars to have a one-piece body shell instead of a chassis with a body built on top.

**Amazing!** Even as late as 1931, some cars ran on steam power. Abner Doble built his first steam car in 1905, and went on to make several luxurious examples. They had plenty of power, and ran almost silently, but at prices between $8,000 and $11,000, they were beyond the reach of the average motorist.

## What was the people's car?

The people's car was the first Volkswagen (which means 'people's car' in German). It was designed in the 1930s by Doctor Ferdinand Porsche to be a small family car which was cheap to run. It was soon nicknamed the Beetle or Bug. 40 million have been made.

Volkswagen Beetle

## Is it true?

*Some cars have armour.*

**YES.** An armoured car is a military vehicle with steel plates on its body to make it bullet-proof. It usually has a small gun, too. Security companies often use vans with armour to transport valuable items or cash. Some limousines also have armour plating to make them bullet proof.

## ❓ Which car could really fly?

In 1949, American inventor Molt Taylor built a car which could be turned into an aeroplane. By 1953, the car had flown over 40,250 kilometres. On the ground, the Aerocar towed its tail and wings in a trailer.

Airborne Aerocar

Aerocar without wings

## ✅ Is it true?

*American cars had the biggest fins of all.*

**YES.** In the 1950s, American car designers began adding pointy bits, such as tail fins, to their cars. Some features were copied from the jet fighters of the time! Tail fins often had rows of lights up the back. These huge and thirsty cars also had plenty of chrome bodywork.

## ❗ Amazing!

 The driver of a Cadillac Coupe de Ville did not have to worry about blinding other drivers with his or her headlights. The car had an electronic eye which detected headlights coming in the opposite direction and automatically dipped its headlights.

## ? Which car had gull wings?

The doors on the 1952 Mercedes 300SL opened upwards like a seagull's wings. The idea was given up because they couldn't be opened if the car turned over in an accident.

Mercedes gull-wing

## ? What was a T-bird?

T-bird was the nickname given to the Ford Thunderbird. The first model appeared in 1953. It was a huge two-seater convertible. In the 1950s, American manufacturers built many huge gas guzzlers like the Thunderbird.

Ford Thunderbird

## ? Who drove around in a bubble?

The owners of small three-wheeled cars made in the 1950s and 1960s drove in bubbles. Their cars were nicknamed 'bubble cars' because of their rounded shape. The front of a bubble car opened for the passengers to get in and out.

BMW Isetta bubble car

## ? What is a smart car?

The Smart car is a joint venture between watch-makers Swatch and Mercedes Benz. It's only 2.5 metres long, and weighs 680 kilograms. Its tiny size makes it the ideal car in congested cities.

Smart car

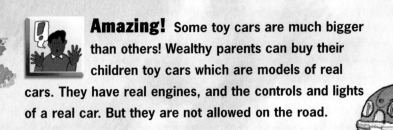

**Amazing!** Some toy cars are much bigger than others! Wealthy parents can buy their children toy cars which are models of real cars. They have real engines, and the controls and lights of a real car. But they are not allowed on the road.

Morris Mini Minor

## Is it true?
*Cars can be stretched.*

**YES.** A car is stretched by cutting it in two and adding an extra piece in the middle. The longest cars in the world are luxurious stretch limousines.

## What is a Mini?

The Mini is a tiny British car, which was designed by the famous car designer Alec Issigonis. It was launched in 1959, and became very fashionable in the 1960s. Many Minis were bought by film actors and pop stars.

51

## ? What is a sports car?

A sports car is a car designed for fast, fun driving. Sports cars have powerful engines for swift acceleration and high top speeds, plus wide tyres for plenty of grip. They often have only two seats and very little luggage space.

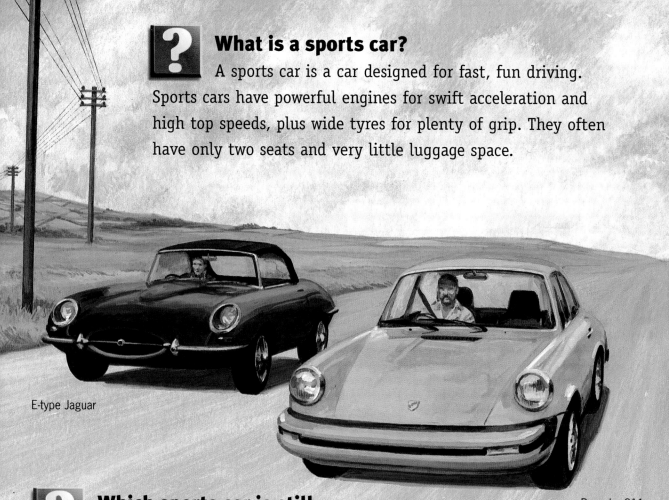

E-type Jaguar

Porsche 911

## ? Which sports car is still hand-made?

Morgan sports cars are still hand built at their factory in Malvern, England. Although they look old fashioned, they can compete with any modern sports car.

Morgan Plus Eight

 **Amazing!** The Austin-Healey Sprite sports car looked like a frog from the front! With its bulging headlights and cheeky smiling radiator grille, this popular classic soon earned the name 'Frogeye' after its launch in 1958.

## Is it true?

*Drophead is a term for a car with a roof that drops off.*

**NO.** Drophead is another word for convertible or cabriolet. The roof can be folded back either by hand, or with an electric motor. Roofless motoring is very popular in countries with a warm climate.

Ferrari 360 Modena

Lotus Elise

## Which powerful car was named after a wild horse?

The Ford Mustang was named after the North American wild horse, or mustang. It was launched in 1964, and was a big hit because of its performance and low cost.

Ford Mustang

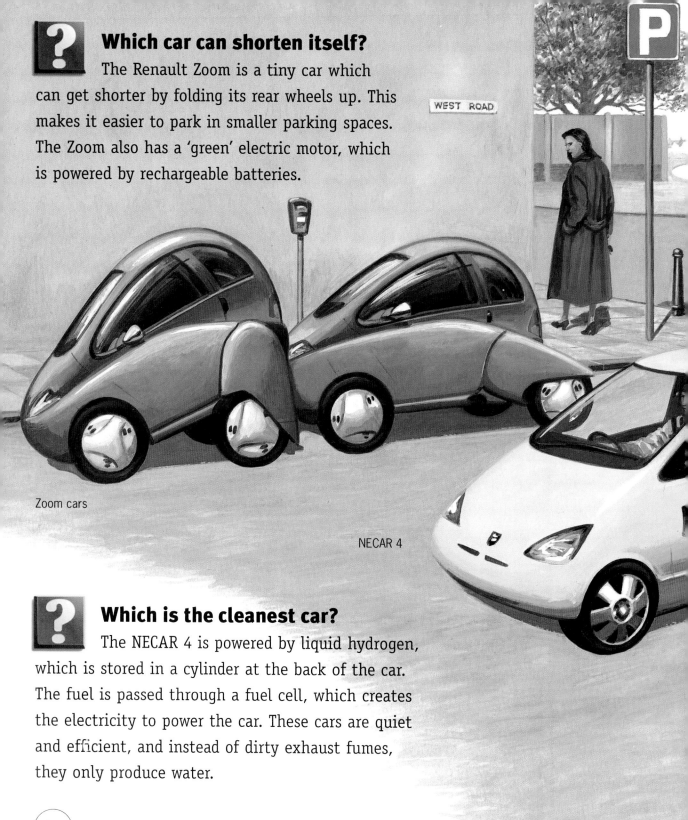

## ? Which car can shorten itself?

The Renault Zoom is a tiny car which can get shorter by folding its rear wheels up. This makes it easier to park in smaller parking spaces. The Zoom also has a 'green' electric motor, which is powered by rechargeable batteries.

WEST ROAD

Zoom cars

NECAR 4

## ? Which is the cleanest car?

The NECAR 4 is powered by liquid hydrogen, which is stored in a cylinder at the back of the car. The fuel is passed through a fuel cell, which creates the electricity to power the car. These cars are quiet and efficient, and instead of dirty exhaust fumes, they only produce water.

## Is it true?

*Cars can run on plants.*

**YES.** In Brazil there's an alternative source of fuel, taken directly from a plant. One 'petrol tree' is able to produce nearly 20 litres of fuel. The Brazilians are planning to grow huge plantations of these trees to solve the problem of increasing fuel shortages.

## Which car runs on sunlight?

Cars are being developed which can convert sunlight into electricity to power their engines. The solar-powered car of the future might look like the vehicle pictured below, with solar panels on the roof.

Prototype solar car

# CHAPTER FOUR

# TRAINS

## ? Which train was pulled by horses?

Between 1800 and 1825, there were 'trains' without engines in Wales and Austria. Horses pulled carriages along the rails. It was a smoother ride than road travel.

## ? Which train was the first to carry passengers?

Stephenson's Locomotion was the first engine to be used on a public railway, the Stockton and Darlington, in 1825. Stephenson's Rocket won £500 in a competition at Rainhill, Liverpool, four years later.

Locomotion

Trevithick's Catch Me Who Can, 1808

## What was the first train engine?

Richard Trevithick, a mine engineer, first demonstrated a mobile engine on rails in 1804. It pulled 70 men and 10 tonnes of iron ore, in front of a crowd of amazed onlookers. His next engine became a fairground ride.

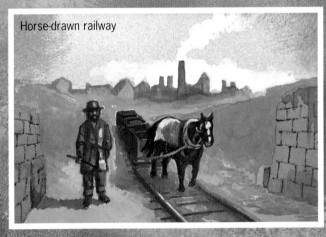

Horse-drawn railway

 **Amazing!** There were horse-drawn trains 50 years ago! The Fintona Branch of Ireland's Great Northern railway remained horse-powered until the early 1950s.

 **Is it true?**
The ancient Greeks had a steam engine!

**YES.** Hero of Alexandria wrote about a steam-powered spinning ball, called the 'aeolipile' in 200 BC. But since slave labour was free, no one bothered to use the engine as a labour-saving device.

Boiler    Smoke stack

Piston

## How is the steam made?

Steam trains all need a fireperson, who shovels coal, or similar fuel, into a firebox. The heat of the fire boils the water, which turns to steam. Smoke from the fire puffs out of the funnel on the smoke stack.

## How does steam power work?

A steam engine is like a big kettle. It uses the pressure of steam to push against pistons inside cylinders. The pistons move sliding rods called linkages, which turn the wheels and make the train move.

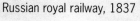
Russian royal railway, 1837

**Amazing!** Russia's first railway was just for royal holidays! The Tsar of Russia had three locomotives made for him in 1837. They ran on a private line from his palace to a royal resort.

## Is it true?

*Steam trains could do 200 kph.*

**YES.** In 1938, a steam engine called Mallard reached 202.7 kph, while pulling a 240 tonne train. That's still a record for a steam engine. It had been souped-up by Herbert Gresley, doubling its power. Mallard is now in a museum in York.

## When was steam power used?

The golden age of steam was from about 1850, until as late as 1950. Since then, steam trains have disappeared from industrial countries, where they only survive as tourist attractions. Steam locomotives still do most of the hard work in many developing countries.

Patrick Stirling's
Single locomotive

61

## Which diesel was a 'centipede'?

America's Pennsylvania Railroad used Baldwin diesel engines in pairs. Each one had 12 small wheels on each side. Linked together, making a 6,000 horse-power monster, they looked like they had 24 'legs'.

1924 Kitson-Still

**Amazing!** Diesel engines can be steam engines too. The 1924 Kitson-Still used a diesel engine for its main power, but also used the heat of the engine to create steam. This powered an extra set of drive wheels.

## Why did diesel take over from steam?

Diesel power first came into use to cope with the problem of smoke in cities and underground railways. During World War Two, military diesel engines became lighter and smaller. Just like today's trains, the engines fitted under the floors of the carriages.

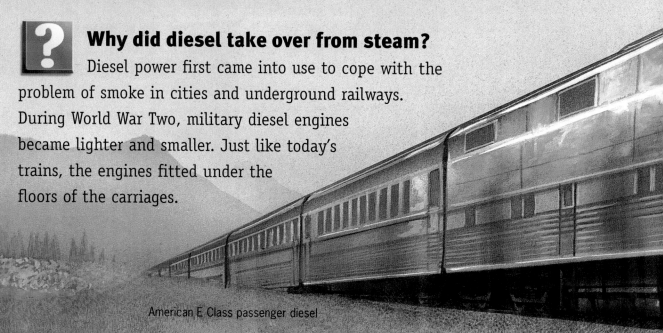

American E Class passenger diesel

## Which diesel looked like an aeroplane?

The German Kruckenburg of 1931 had a huge propeller at the back which pushed it along like an aeroplane on rails. It reached speeds up to 230 kph during a 10-kilometre speed trial. Unfortunately, it was too noisy and dangerous for everyday use.

1931 Kruckenburg

## Is it true?

*Diesel engines use electric motors.*

**YES.** Many diesel-engined trains actually use electric motors to turn the wheels. The engine itself uses diesel fuel. It turns a generator, which creates the electricity needed by the electric motors. This is because electric motors turn powerfully at all speeds, unlike a diesel engine.

von Siemens' electric train

**YES.** Werner von Siemens demonstrated an electric train at the Berlin Trades Exhibition, in Germany in 1879. People queued up to have a ride on the tiny carriages.

## ? Which country went electric first?

France was the first country to use electric trains on a major mainline route, making the whole of the Paris to Orléans route electric in 1900. French electric trains have broken many speed records. This 1981 train was able to travel as fast as 380 kph, which was a record at the time.

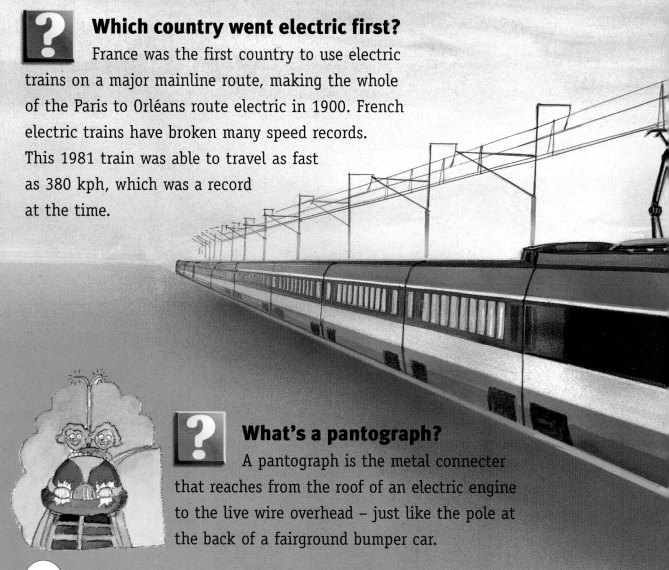

## ? What's a pantograph?

A pantograph is the metal connecter that reaches from the roof of an electric engine to the live wire overhead – just like the pole at the back of a fairground bumper car.

**Amazing!** One electric train travels all over Europe. Trans-Europ-Express was designed to use the different electricity supplies in different European countries. Engineers have to change its wheels, though, every time it travels in and out of Spain.

Underground train

## ? Are electric engines better than diesel?

Electric power lets trains use energy without creating too much mess. The only pollution is at the power station where the electricity is made. Electric power is ideal for trams and underground trains in cities. Diesels are better on long routes where great lengths of electricity would be too expensive.

French TGV high-speed train, 1981

Tunnel-boring machine

 ## Is the Channel Tunnel longest?

Not quite. The Channel Tunnel is 49.8 kilometres in total. The Seikan, Japan's tunnel between the main islands of Honshu and Hokkaido, travels an amazing 53.9 kilometres underground.

Royal Albert Bridge, spanning the River Tamar, England

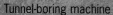 ## How do trains cross rivers?

Trains use big bridges or deep tunnels to cross the largest rivers. The Victorian engineer, Isambard Kingdom Brunel, invented strong metal bridges to carry the weight of a train. Some bridges are so big that repainting them is a full-time job!

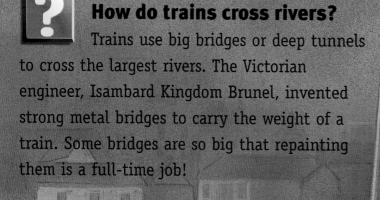

## ❓ Where was the first raised city railway?

New York City had a serious traffic problem in the 1880s, and that was before cars! An 'Elevated Railway', known as 'the L' for short, was built above the streets. It still works today.

New York Elevated Railway

**Amazing!** You can take a train on a boat. Train ferries started operating in the late 1800s between England and France. Passengers stayed in their seats all the way from London to Paris!

**Is it true?**
*Box Hill tunnel knows its creator's birthday.*

**YES.** Brunel built it at a special angle. Each year, only on his birthday, the sun shines right through the entire 3.2 kilometre tunnel in southern England.

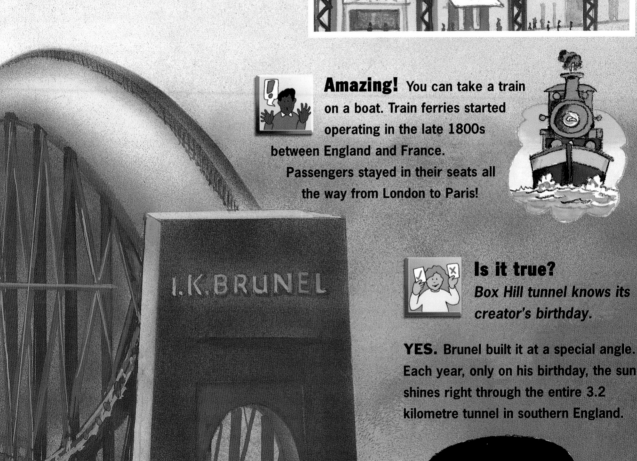

I.K.BRUNEL

## How long is the longest train?

The longest train ever was a freight train measuring 7.3 kilometres! The longest passenger train was a measly 1.7 kilometres, but the Belgian railway couldn't find a platform long enough to park it!

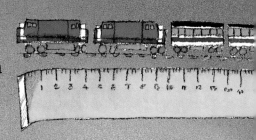

Track laying

Modern TGV

**Amazing!** Eight men can lay 16 kilometres of track in a day! A team of eight track layers in America set this world record on April 18, 1869.

## Which train is fastest?

France pioneered fast trains after World War Two. When Japan introduced the Shinkansen 'bullet train' in the 1960s, France responded with the TGV. An experimental TGV has reached 515 kph!

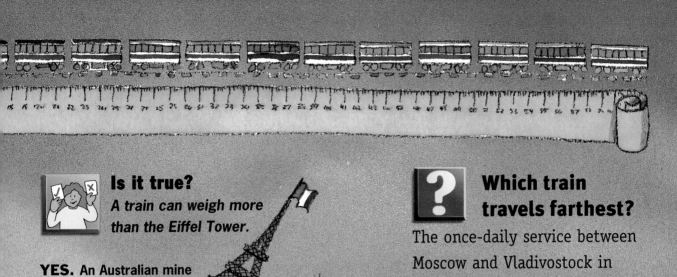

## Is it true?

*A train can weigh more than the Eiffel Tower.*

**YES.** An Australian mine train was weighed in 1996 at 72,191 tonnes – that's more than eight Eiffel Towers!

## Which train travels farthest?

The once-daily service between Moscow and Vladivostock in Russia travels 9,350 kilometres, taking eight days. Known as the Trans-Siberian Express, or The Russia, the train has featured in several books and films.

Trans-Siberian Express

## Which train flies?

Really fast future trains might not bother with wheels. They could ride on a cushion of air, like a hovercraft. The nose of the train squashes air underneath its belly as it jets along, and the squashed air lifts it above the ground. The Aerotrain already exists as an experimental vehicle.

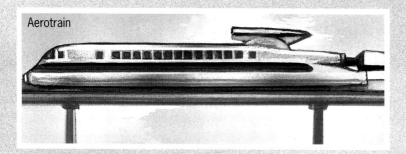

Aerotrain

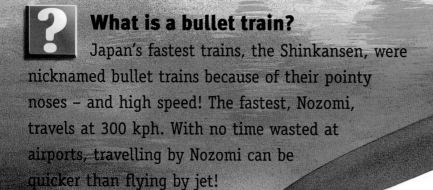

**Amazing!** One sled travelled at Mach 8. An unmanned rocket vehicle on rails achieved 9,851 kph in an American experiment in 1982. On straight track, it could make the eight-day Trans-Siberian trip in less than one hour!

## What is a bullet train?

Japan's fastest trains, the Shinkansen, were nicknamed bullet trains because of their pointy noses – and high speed! The fastest, Nozomi, travels at 300 kph. With no time wasted at airports, travelling by Nozomi can be quicker than flying by jet!

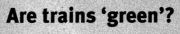
## Are trains 'green'?

Trains are less harmful to the environment than most other kinds of transport. They are particularly important in cities, where underground trains, trams and monorails can reduce pollution from cars, buses and taxis. For long distance journeys, trains use much less fuel than jet aircraft.

### Is it true?
*Some trains run on magnets.*

**YES.** Germany and Japan have both tested trains that use repelling magnets to float above the track. The track doesn't wear out, and the trains can slip along at amazing speeds.

JR500 Shinkansen bullet train

71

## CHAPTER FIVE

# MOTORBIKES

Michaux-Perreaux 1869

 ## Which bike had a steam engine?

The Michaux-Perreaux bicycle of 1869 had a steam engine under its saddle. Wood or coal had to be put in the engine every few minutes to keep the water boiling, to work the engine.

 ## Who put an engine above a front wheel?

The Werner brothers in France built a motorcycle in 1899. It was a safety bicycle with a petrol engine above the front wheel, in front of the handlebars.

Werner 1899

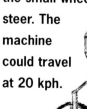 ## Amazing!

American engineer Lucius Copeland made a motorcycle by adding a small steam engine to a penny farthing. He rode the bicycle backwards, using the small wheel to steer. The machine could travel at 20 kph.

## ? What did the first motorbike look like?

The first proper motorbike had a heavy wooden frame, wooden wheels with metal rims, and two stabilising wheels to stop it toppling over. It was the first motorbike to have a lightweight petrol engine, but it was very slow. It was built by German engineers Daimler and Maybach in 1885.

Daimler/Maybach 1885

### Is it true?
*Early motorcycles had pedals.*

**YES.** The engines on early motorcycles were not very powerful or reliable. So the bikes had pedals for going up hills or in case of a breakdown. Some modern bikes, such as mopeds, still have pedals.

## ? Who were Harley and Davidson?

William, Walter and Arthur Davidson, along with William Harley, founded Harley-Davidson in 1903. Their first bike went into production the following year.

1912 Harley-Davidson

**Amazing!** The Italian company Moto Guzzi, founded in the 1920s, borrowed the eagle-shaped badge of the Italian Air Force to put on their bikes.

1930 Brough Superior

1928 Indian 101 Scout

## ? Why was Brough superior?

British engineer George Brough designed one of the best and most expensive bikes of all time, and called it the Brough Superior. It was known as the 'Rolls-Royce of motorbikes'. The most famous owner of a Brough Superior was the British war hero Lawrence of Arabia.

## What was an Indian?

Indian was a famous American company which manufactured motorbikes in the first half of the 20th century. One of Indian's most successful bikes was the Indian Scout, which appeared in 1920 and was manufactured for 30 years. It had a 600 cc engine, shaft drive, and a top speed of 121 kph.

## Is it true?

*Rollie Free rode a Vincent Black Shadow in a swimming costume.*

**YES.** The Vincent Black Shadow was the first motorbike to reach over 250 kph. It did it in 1948, and its rider, Rollie Free, wore just a swimming costume and rode lying flat to reduce air drag. If he had sat upright on the saddle, he wouldn't have reached this speed.

## ? What is a hog?

Hog is the nickname for a Harley-Davidson motorbike. One of the best and most famous hogs was the Harley-Davidson Electra Glide, often used by the highway patrols of American police forces.

1988
Harley-Davidson
Electra Glide

1982 Honda
Gold Wing with
sidecar and
trailer

**Amazing!** Carl Stevens Clancy rode around the world on a motorbike in 1912, the first person to achieve this feat. His 29,000-kilometre journey started in the USA, and took him through Europe, Africa, Japan, and back home to New York.

## ? What is a sidecar?

A sidecar is a small one-wheeled car that bolts on to the side of a motorbike. It turns the motorbike into a three-wheeled vehicle. The sidecar can carry a passenger or luggage. With a sidecar attached, the bike rider cannot lean over on corners.

### ? What is a Gold Wing?

A Gold Wing is a giant touring bike made by the Japanese company Honda. The Gold Wing is very smooth to ride, has a seat for a passenger, and an engine powerful enough to pull a sidecar and a trailer. It's perfect for long-distance touring.

### Is it true?
*Passengers used to ride in baskets.*

**YES.** The bodies of sidecars for early motorbikes were made of wicker, which was also used to make baskets. Wicker is made by weaving bendy wooden branches together.

79

## Amazing!
Trials bikes can make short hops up almost vertical rock faces. The rider needs good balance and expert control of the clutch and gears.

## Which motorcyclists wear armour?
Riders in motocross races wear tough plastic body armour to protect them in case they fall off, or are hit by other bikes. They also wear long, tough boots, helmets and goggles to keep mud out of their eyes.

## What is a trials bike?
Trials bikes are designed for riding on steep, rough and rocky ground. They are ridden in motorbike trials, where riders have to ride over obstacles without stopping or putting their feet down to balance.

Trials bike

**NO.** Riders often take part in motocross competitions held in deserts. There are also long-distance desert motorbike rallies, such as the Paris-Dakar Rally which crosses the dusty Sahara Desert.

Paris-Dakar Rally

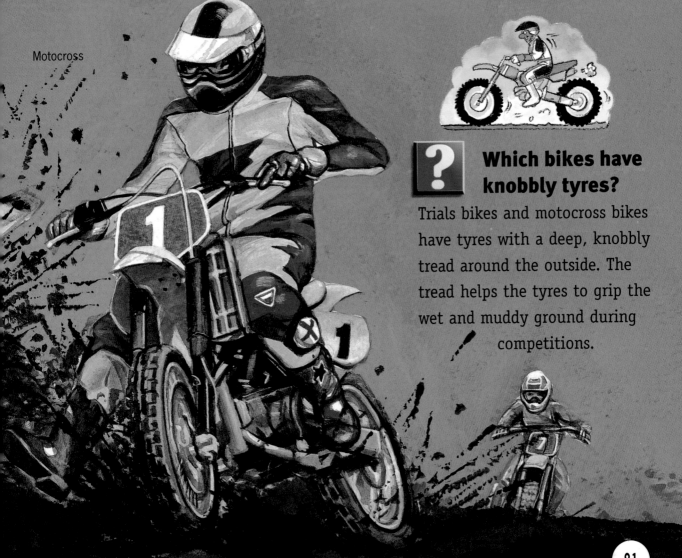

Motocross

### Which bikes have knobbly tyres?

Trials bikes and motocross bikes have tyres with a deep, knobbly tread around the outside. The tread helps the tyres to grip the wet and muddy ground during competitions.

1942 Harley-Davidson WLA

## Who had a holster on a Harley?

US Army despatch riders of World War Two carried a rifle in a holster on their Harley-Davidson WLA 45 motorbikes. More than 80,000 WLAs were made during the war, and many of them were bought by ex-soldiers afterwards.

## Is it true?
*The first US soldier to enter Germany after the First World War rode a Harley?*

**YES.** Corporal Holtz, an American soldier, was photographed riding into Germany on a Harley with sidecar, the day after the war ended in 1918.

## Who dropped from the sky with mini bikes?

During World War Two, when some Allied and German soldiers jumped from their aircraft, their mini motorbikes parachuted down with them.

German mini-scooter

**Amazing!** In World War Two the German army used a vehicle called a Ketten Kraftrad that was half motorbike, half armoured car. It had a motorbike front wheel and caterpillar tracks.

## Who had machine guns on their motorbikes?

German World War Two soldiers rode high-speed BMW motorcycles with sidecars. One soldier operated the heavy machine gun in the sidecar.

BMW R-75

## ? What is a TT race?

TT races are held every year on the public roads of the Isle of Man, part of the British Isles. TT stands for Tourist Trophy because, when the races started in 1907, they were for touring motorbikes.

Norton Isle of Man TT racer

1915 Harley-Davidson

## ? Who raced on wooden boards?

Early motorcycle races used to take place on wooden bicycle tracks. Imagine the splinters if you fell off!

### Is it true?
*All motorbikes have brakes.*

**NO.** Motorbikes built for speedway racing have no brakes, and only one gear. These races take place on oval tracks made of dirt, sand, grass, and sometimes ice. The riders slide round the bends at each end of the track.

**Amazing!** In high-speed crashes, motorbike racers sometimes skid across the ground at 250 kph! So racers wear leather overalls to protect them in case they fall off. They also have tough knee pads sewn into their leathers because their knees touch the road as they lean into bends.

## What is a superbike?

A superbike, such as this Ducati, is a very fast motorbike, normally with an engine of 750 cc or bigger. The word 'superbike' was first used to describe the Honda CB750 of the late 1960s. Superbikes are designed for high-speed racing but can also be used for touring on public roads.

Ducati superbike

## ❓ What is stunt riding?

Stunt riders speed up ramps on their bikes, and jump over cars, buses and trucks. The most famous stunt rider of all, Evel Knievel, even tried to jump a canyon in a rocket-powered 'skycycle' in 1974. He nearly drowned in the attempt. Evel claims that he has broken every bone in his body!

Evel Knievel

 **Amazing!**
Teams of stunt riders perform incredible tricks such as building motorcycle pyramids and jumping through rings of fire. For a pyramid, the team members balance on each other's shoulders while the bikes are moving.

Wall of death

## ❓ What is the wall of death?

The wall of death is a circular, vertical wall. Stunt riders whizz round and round it on their motorbikes, as if they're riding inside a tin can! They have to ride at full speed to stop falling off the wall.

**NO.** Riders can lift their front wheels off the ground and ride along on the rear wheel. This trick is called a wheelie. Superbike racers do wheelies to celebrate winning a race.

## ? What is freestyle motocross?

Freestyle motocross is a new motorbike sport where the riders perform daring tricks as they jump off humps on a dirt track. Sometimes they even let go of their bikes completely!

Freestyle motocross

# CHAPTER SIX

# TRUCKS

## Which trucks had steam engines?

In the 19th century, the first powered trucks had steam engines, before petrol engines and diesel engines were invented. They looked like the steam tractors used on farms.

Foden steam truck

**Amazing!** The first ever steam-powered vehicle was destroyed in a crash. The three-wheeled carriage was built by French engineer Nicolas-Joseph Cugnot in 1769, and was supposed to pull artillery guns.

## What did trucks look like before steam engines were invented?

Before steam engines were invented, cargo was moved in wagons pulled by animals such as oxen or horses. This is why the first powered trucks and cars were called 'horseless' carriages.

Wagon train

## What was a charabanc?

A charabanc was a flat-bodied truck with benches in the back for passengers to sit on. Factory workers and their families travelled in charabancs on days out to the seaside or to the city. The first charabancs were pulled by teams of horses.

Charabanc

## Is it true?

*Early buses were pulled by steam tractors.*

**YES.** A steam tractor was a steam-powered vehicle designed for towing wagons. The first passenger-carrying buses were made up of a wagon with several seats inside, pulled by a steam tractor.

91

Cab-over truck

**YES.** The diesel engine, which is a type of internal combustion engine, was first demonstrated by German engineer Rudolph Diesel in 1897. Most trucks have diesel engines because they are usually more economical and more reliable than petrol engines.

## What is a cab-over truck?

A cab-over truck is a truck where the driver's cab is over the top of the engine. The whole cab tips forwards so that a mechanic can reach the engine to repair it.

## What is the fifth wheel?

The fifth wheel is the swivelling connecting device on all articulated trucks, behind the cab on the tractor unit. Trailers link on to it. The fifth wheel lets the trailer swivel when the truck turns corners.

Fifth wheel

## What gives piggy-back rides?

Truck tractor units are often delivered by being towed by another truck as though they were trailers. It saves money because the trucks being towed don't use up any fuel.

Kenworth piggy-back trucks

## What is a monster truck?

A monster truck is an ordinary pick-up truck fitted with huge dump-truck wheels, extra-strong suspension and a very powerful engine. Monster truck owners race their trucks over tracks with huge bumps and jumps. The trucks bounce about and even tip over if they go too quickly.

Monster truck

### Is it true?

*Monster trucks drive over cars.*

**YES.** In monster truck racing, some of the obstacles that the trucks drive over are old cars! The cars get crushed flat under the trucks' massive wheels.

Bedford Afghan truck

Customised pick-up truck

## Who paints trucks for protection?

In countries such as Afghanistan and India, truck drivers paint their trucks with bright colours and religious symbols. They believe that the symbols will stop them from having accidents.

**Amazing!** One of most famous American monster trucks is called Grave Digger. It has an amazing custom paint job, with scenes of graveyards all over its bodywork!

## What are customised trucks?

Customised trucks have special parts such as huge wheels, high suspensions and big engines. Some even have boots, bonnets and doors moved by hydraulic rams. Custom trucks are built specially for shows and races.

95

## ? What is a dragster truck?

A dragster truck is customised for high-acceleration drag racing. Dragsters race against each other in pairs from a standing start along a short track. Dragsters have extra-powerful engines and enormous rear tyres to get plenty of grip on the road.

Dragster trucks

Hawaiian Fire Department's jet truck

## ? What is the fastest truck?

The world's fastest truck is the Hawaiian Fire Department's custom built fire truck. This truck was originally built in 1940, and is powered by two jet engines taken from aircraft! It can reach more than 650 kilometres per hour.

## Is it true?
*You can race trucks.*

**YES.** There's lots of truck racing around the world. In the USA, drivers race customised pick-up trucks. In Europe, they race big truck tractor units.

Leyland truck doing a wheelie

## ? Can trucks do wheelies?

Customised pick-up trucks can do wheelies. They have huge engines and a heavy weight at the rear to help the front rise up.

## How do tanks travel?

Tanks are good at driving across rough, muddy ground, but they're quite slow. When tanks need to move quickly, they're carried on special tank transporters. The transporter's trailer needs lots of wheels to spread out the huge weight of the tank.

Oshkosh tank transporter

Amphibious trucks

## Which trucks can swim?

Armies transport equipment in amphibious trucks that can drive on land like a normal truck and float across water like a boat. Amphibious trucks have a waterproof underside to stop water flooding the engine.

**Amazing!** Some trucks have armour plating on the outside. They're called armoured personnel carriers (APCs for short). They're used to carry troops on battlefields.

Russian mobile missile launcher

## ? What carries missiles?

Missile-carrying trucks transport huge nuclear missiles. On board the truck is a launch pad and a control centre for launching the missile. The trucks carry the missiles into the countryside if their base is threatened by enemy attack.

 **Is it true?**
*Some trucks have caterpillar tracks.*

**YES.** A type of truck called a half-track has wheels at the front and caterpillar tracks at the rear. Armies often transport their troops in half-tracks.

## ? Which truck scrapes?

A scraper is a truck that scrapes a thin layer of soil from the ground and collects it. Scrapers move and level earth during road building.

Scraper

Excavator

## ? What is a digger?

A digger is machine that digs holes in the ground with a bucket on the end of an arm. The arm and bucket are moved by powerful hydraulic rams. Caterpillar tracks help the digger move across rough, muddy ground. Some diggers are called excavators.

 **Is it true?**
Digger buckets can hold two cars.

**YES.** Massive diggers that work in quarries and open-cast mines gouge rock and earth out with huge rotating bucket wheels. Each bucket could hold two cars.

## Which is the biggest truck in the world?

The world's biggest truck is a dumper truck called a Terex Titan. It's as tall as a house and carries 300 tonnes of rubble. Each of its tyres is twice as high as a person.

Terex Titan

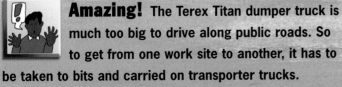

**Amazing!** The Terex Titan dumper truck is much too big to drive along public roads. So to get from one work site to another, it has to be taken to bits and carried on transporter trucks.

## How do loggers load logs?

Log-carrying trucks have a small crane on the back with a strong grab on the end. The driver controls the grab, which lifts whole tree trunks stripped of their branches on to the truck. Bars on the trailer stop the logs rolling off.

 **Amazing!** Big car transporters can carry up to a dozen cars at once. They have cleverly designed decks and ramps which allow the cars to drive on and off, and fold up so the cars fit into a tiny space.

Logger

 **Is it true?**
*Tankers carry chocolate.*

**NO.** But tanker trucks can carry almost anything liquid, including milk and oil, and solids such as flour.

## What is a road train?

A truck with two or more trailers is called a road train because it looks like a train travelling on the road. Road trains have powerful tractor units and a big sleeper cab. They are used mainly in Australia.

Straddle truck

## What is a straddle truck?

A straddle truck is a type of mobile crane. It rolls over the load it is going to lift, with wheels on each side of the load. Straddle trucks often work in ports, lifting and moving cargo containers.

ROAD TRAIN

Australian road train

# CHAPTER SEVEN

# AIRCRAFT

## ? Who made the first aeroplane flight?

The first person to make a controlled flight in an aeroplane with an engine was Orville Wright. His flight took place in the aeroplane Flyer on December 17, 1903, at Kitty Hawk, North Carolina, USA. The flight lasted just 12 seconds and was 36.5 metres long. Flyer was a biplane built by Orville and his brother Wilbur, who were bicycle makers.

Antoinette monoplane

Flyer

 **Amazing!** In 1914, the fastest aircraft were slower than the fastest racing cars. The world speed record for aircraft was just over 204 kilometres per hour, but the world land-speed record was 226 kilometres per hour. By 1920, aircraft had overtaken.

## What is a monoplane?

A monoplane is an aeroplane with one pair of wings. Most early aeroplanes were biplanes, with two sets of wings. The graceful Antoinette VII of 1908 was one of the first monoplanes to fly.

### Is it true?
*One plane had 20 wings.*

**YES.** In 1904 Englishman Horatio Phillips built a plane with 20 small wings one above the other. It was a complete failure. In 1907 he built a plane with no less than 200 wings!

Blériot XI

## Who was first to fly across the English Channel?

The first cross-channel flight was made by Frenchman Louis Blériot in 1909. He made the trip in one of his own aeroplanes, a Blériot number XI monoplane. It took just 37 minutes to fly from France to England. Blériot won a prize of £1,000.

## ❓ Which airship burst into flames?

The hydrogen-filled airship Hindenburg exploded in 1937, killing 35 of the 97 people on board. It was one of the two largest airships ever. It was 245 metres long. That's two and a half soccer pitches!

Hindenburg

Giffard's airship

## ❓ Who flew the first airship?

Frenchman Henri Giffard flew the first airship in 1852. It had a propeller driven by a small steam engine. Giffard travelled 27 kilometres at 8 kph.

## Amazing!

In 1802 Frenchman André Jacques Garnerin jumped from the basket of his hot-air balloon above London. He floated safely down under a parachute. It was the first successful parachute jump.

Breitling Orbiter

## Is it true?

*The first non-stop round-the-world balloon flight was in 1999.*

**YES.** Bertrand Piccard and Brian Jones flew the Breitling Orbiter 3 from Chateaux D'Oex in Switzerland, and crossed the finishing line in Mauritania 19 days, 21 hours and 55 minutes later. Piccard and Jones finally landed in the Egyptian desert.

## Are airships used today?

Today small airships fly above major sporting events. They carry television cameras to give viewers a bird's eye view of the action. They often have huge advertising displays on their sides.

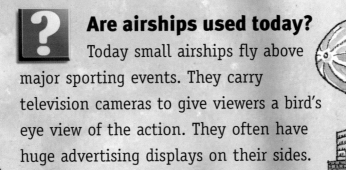

## ? Who was the Red Baron?

The greatest fighter ace of the
First World War, Baron Manfred von
Richthofen, was known as the Red Baron.
Between 1916 and 1918 he shot down 80
allied aircraft. He got his nickname from
the bright red Fokker Dr I triplane
he often flew in combat.

The Red Baron's Fokker Dr I triplane

**! Amazing!** Some fighter
pilots were not allowed to wear
parachutes! During the First
World War, the commanders of the British
Royal Flying Corps banned pilots, gunners
and navigators from carrying parachutes
to escape from crippled aircraft.

Vickers Vimy

## Is it true?

*Pilots shot at their own propellers.*

**YES.** During the First World War, pilots fired machine guns at their own propellers. To start with, propellers were protected by metal plates. In 1915, a system was invented that made sure that the gun fired only when a propeller blade was not in the way.

Curtiss JN-4 'Jenny'

## What were barnstormers?

Barnstormers were stunt pilots. They toured the USA in the 1920s, performing daredevil flying stunts, such as hanging from their biplanes by their teeth. They also gave rides to the public. Barnstormers got their name by flying very low over farm buildings.

## Who were the first people to fly across the Atlantic?

The first people to fly non-stop across the Atlantic were Britons Captain John Alcock and Lieutenant Arthur Whitten Brown. They flew in a twin-engined Vickers Vimy bomber, in 1919. It took 16 hours and 17 minutes and ended with a crash into a bog!

111

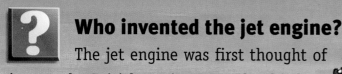

## Who invented the jet engine?

The jet engine was first thought of in 1930 by British engineer Frank Whittle. By 1937 he had built a working jet engine. At the same time in Germany Hans von Ohain was building a similar engine.

de Havilland Comet

Heinkel He 178

**Amazing!** When the first jet-powered aeroplane took off on its maiden flight, it sucked a bird into its engine. The plane was the Heinkel He 178. All modern jet engines are designed to withstand 'bird strikes', which could snap off the engine's fan blades and cause a crash.

## What was the first jet plane?

The first two jet planes were experimental fighters built during the Second World War. The German Heinkel He 178 flew in 1939 and the British Gloster E 28/39 in 1941.

Gloster E28/39

## What was the first jet airliner?

The first jet airliner to carry passengers was the de Havilland Comet I. It had four jet engines set into the wing roots. The first airline service using the Comet was begun in 1952 by the British Overseas Airways Corporation, between London and Johannesburg.

## Is it true?

*Jet engines have fans.*

**YES.** At the front of a jet engine there is an enormous fan which sucks in air. Large airliners have jet engines called turbofans, with fans as tall as a person. The fan compresses the air and forces it into the engine. Fuel burns in the air, creating a rush of hot gases which blast out of the engine. They spin a turbine that works the fan.

Air pulled in and compressed by front fans

Compressed air and fuel burnt in combustion chamber

Exhaust provides thrust

## Is it true?

*The first jet-to-jet combat took place during the Second World War.*

**NO.** Jet fighters started flying on both sides near the end of the Second World War, but they never met in combat. The first time one jet fighter fought another was in 1950, during the Korean War. A USAF Lockheed F-80C shot down a Chinese MiG-15.

## ? Which fighter can swing its wings?

The Panavia Tornado has 'swing' wings that can pivot backwards and forwards. The forward position is for take-off and landing because it gives plenty of lift when the aeroplane is moving slowly. After take-off the wings are swept back for high-speed flight.

Panavia Tornado

## Amazing!

Fighter aircraft often fill up their fuel tanks while they are in the air. This is called in-flight refuelling. The fuel comes from a large tanker aircraft. The fighter and tanker pilots have to fly very skilfully to connect up with the fuel hose dangling behind the tanker.

Stealth fighter

## Which plane is invisible?

The Lockheed F117A Stealth fighter is meant to be invisible to radar systems. The F117A's flat surfaces and special paint help to scatter enemy radar signals, making it very difficult to track. But an American Stealth fighter was downed in Yugoslavia in 1999.

Grumman X-29A

## Which plane has back-to-front wings?

It looks as though the wings of the Grumman X-29A have been put on the wrong way round, but they haven't. The X-29A was built as an experiment. Its wings make it so unstable that it can only be flown by computers.

# Which plane travelled at 7,270 kph?

On 3 October, 1967, an American X-15 rocket-powered aeroplane reached 7,270 kph. It's still the world record speed for an aeroplane. The X-15 also holds the altitude record of 107,960 metres. That's nearly 108 kilometres above the Earth's surface!

X-15 rocket plane

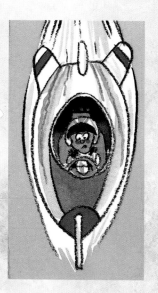

## Which plane had no wings?

In the 1970s, US Air Force pilots flew an experimental plane called the X-24A without wings. This rocket plane had a specially shaped fuselage, or lifting body, to keep airborne.

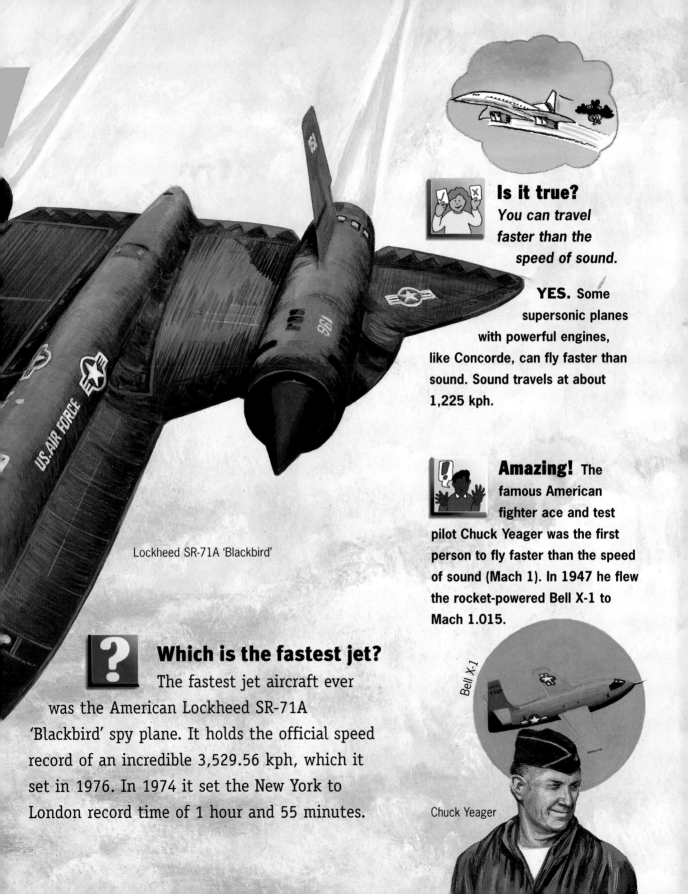

Lockheed SR-71A 'Blackbird'

## Is it true?

*You can travel faster than the speed of sound.*

**YES.** Some supersonic planes with powerful engines, like Concorde, can fly faster than sound. Sound travels at about 1,225 kph.

**Amazing!** The famous American fighter ace and test pilot Chuck Yeager was the first person to fly faster than the speed of sound (Mach 1). In 1947 he flew the rocket-powered Bell X-1 to Mach 1.015.

Bell X-1

Chuck Yeager

## Which is the fastest jet?

The fastest jet aircraft ever was the American Lockheed SR-71A 'Blackbird' spy plane. It holds the official speed record of an incredible 3,529.56 kph, which it set in 1976. In 1974 it set the New York to London record time of 1 hour and 55 minutes.

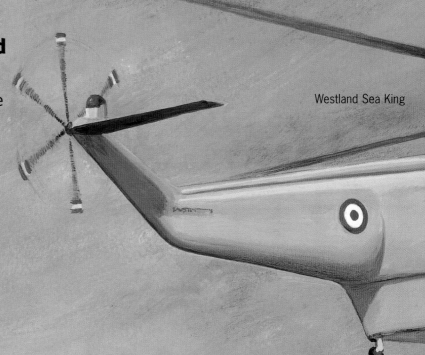

## ? Why are helicopters used for rescuing people?

Helicopters make good rescue aircraft because they can hover in the air and land in small spaces. At sea they hover while the crew pull people from the water. They are also used to lift injured mountaineers to hospital.

Westland Sea King

Sikorsky VS-300

 **Amazing!**
Helicopters can be used as cranes! 'Skycranes' can move heavy objects over short distances. They have a cargo space where the fuselage normally is.

## ? Who invented the first true helicopter?

People had been making brief helicopter flights since 1907, but the first successful helicopter flight was in 1939, when inventor Igor Sikorsky flew his VS-300. This had a single main rotor and a tail rotor, and was the ancestor of all modern helicopters.

118

## Is it true?

*All helicopters have two rotors.*

**NO.** Very modern helicopters have a tail thruster instead of a second rotor, but most helicopters do have two rotors. As the engine spins the main rotor one way, it also tries to spin the fuselage the other way. A second rotor on the tail stops this happening. On twin-rotor helicopters, the main rotors spin in opposite directions, so no tail rotor is needed.

Autogyro

## **?** What is an autogyro?

An autogyro has a rotor that is not driven by an engine. As the autogyro is pushed along by its propeller, the rotor spins round automatically, providing the lift that keeps the autogyro in the air.

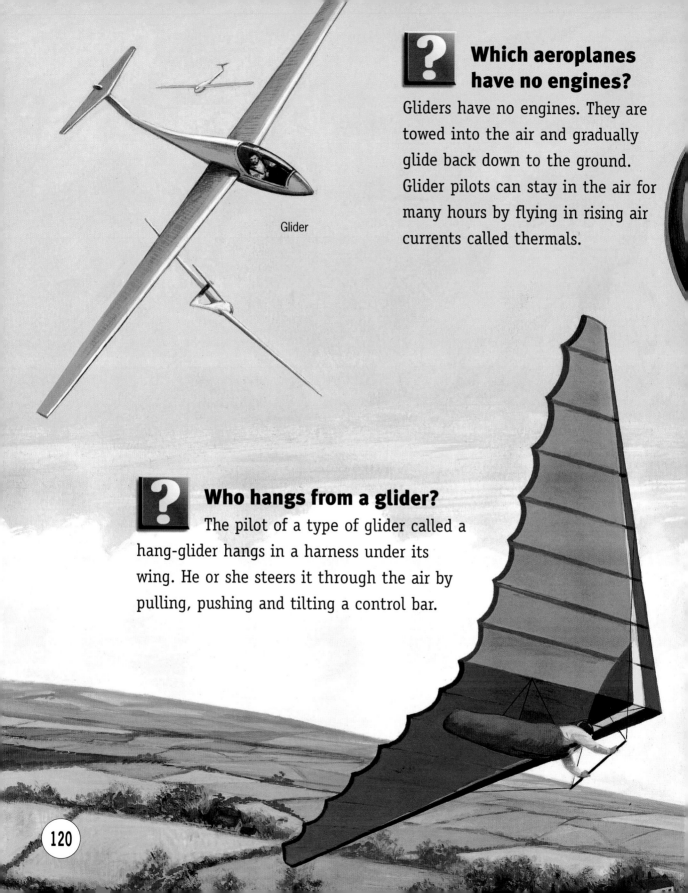

## ? Which aeroplanes have no engines?

Gliders have no engines. They are towed into the air and gradually glide back down to the ground. Glider pilots can stay in the air for many hours by flying in rising air currents called thermals.

Glider

## ? Who hangs from a glider?

The pilot of a type of glider called a hang-glider hangs in a harness under its wing. He or she steers it through the air by pulling, pushing and tilting a control bar.

Hot-air balloon

**Amazing!** Pilots of paragliders can strap tiny engines to their backs to make a tiny plane. A paraglider is a bit like a parachute that fills up with air to make a wing. The pilot hangs in a harness under the wing.

## Who flies on hot air?

Pilots and passengers in hot-air balloons are held up by hot air. A gas burner heats the air inside the balloon, making it hotter and lighter than the color air outside. This makes the balloon float upwards like an air-filled ball under water.

### Is it true?

*The space shuttle is a glider.*

**YES.** The space shuttle is lifted up into space by huge rockets, but lands back on Earth as a glider. The two solid fuel boosters fall away before it returns to Earth, so the pilot only has one chance to get the landing right.

## CHAPTER EIGHT

# SPACECRAFT

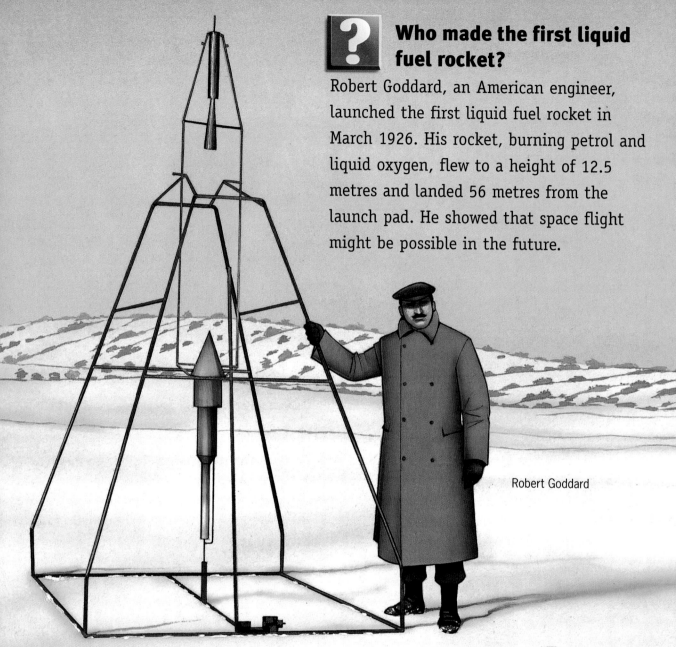

## ? Who made the first liquid fuel rocket?

Robert Goddard, an American engineer, launched the first liquid fuel rocket in March 1926. His rocket, burning petrol and liquid oxygen, flew to a height of 12.5 metres and landed 56 metres from the launch pad. He showed that space flight might be possible in the future.

Robert Goddard

 **Amazing!** The Chinese invented rockets around the beginning of the last millennium! Powered by an early version of gunpowder, Chinese rockets in AD 1000 looked like fireworks. They were used in battle as flaming arrows! For the last 1,000 years, most big advances in rocket design have been made as a result of war.

## What did the first satellite do?

Sputnik 1 was launched into orbit by Soviet Russia on October 4, 1957, 121 days ahead of its American rival, Explorer 1. Sputnik 1 circled the Earth once every 90 minutes for 21 days, sending radio messages which the world listened to on the radio.

Sputnik 1

German V2 rocket

## Is it true?

*Rockets were used in World War Two.*

**YES.** The German scientist Wernher von Braun made rockets that could launch bombs across the English Channel. They damaged London without risking the lives of German pilots. Von Braun's V2 rocket was so successful that after the war America gave him a job helping with its space programme.

## Who was the first earthling in space?

Before the first humans went to space, animals paved the way. Laika, a Russian mongrel dog, was the first earthling in space. Her seven days in orbit proved that space travel would be safe for humans.

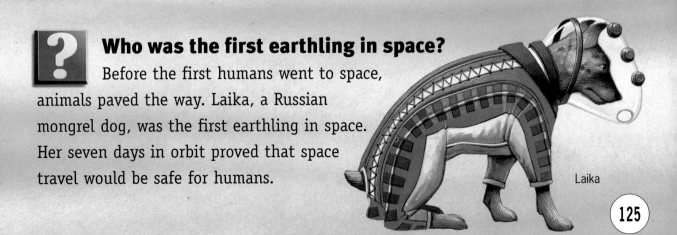

Laika

 ## What was the biggest rocket ever?

American Saturn 5 rockets were 111-metre tall monsters, weighing 2,903 tonnes on the launch pad. That's as heavy as 600 elephants! They were more greedy than elephants, too, burning 15 tonnes of fuel per second. Saturn 5 rockets were used to launch all the Apollo missions to the Moon.

Ariane rocket launching a satellite in space

## What do rockets carry?

Rocket cargo is called the payload, the load that pays for the trip. Most rockets are designed to carry one or two satellites. Some satellites are for scientific research, some are for communication, and some are for spying. Of course, rockets can also carry people!

126

Saturn 5

**Is it true?**
*Jet planes can fly in space.*

**NO.** Jet engines need to take oxygen from the air around them to burn fuel. Because there's no air in space, a jet engine wouldn't work up there.

**?** **Why do rockets have stages?**

Rockets have to be big to carry enough fuel to escape the Earth's pull. But once the fuel is burnt, those big engines and fuel tanks are useless. Their weight would make visiting the Moon very difficult. So rockets are made in stages, or pieces, which drop off when they've done their job.

Saturn 5

**Amazing!** Three German engineers made a rocket-powered car in 1928! Fritz von Opel, Max Valier and Friedrich Sander tested the first version, Opel-Rak 1, on March 15, 1928. Opel later used the rocket knowledge he learnt from Valier to fit 16 rockets on to a glider plane. It was the second ever rocket-powered aircraft.

Launch escape system

Command module

Service module

Lunar module inside

Stage 3 contains fuel and rocket engines

Stage 2 contains fuel and rocket engines

Stage 1 contains fuel and rocket engines

USA   USA

## Who was the first person in space?

Yuri Gagarin, a 27-year-old Soviet pilot, orbited the Earth on April 12, 1961. He spent 90 minutes in space in the Vostok 1 spacecraft before returning safely to Earth. Gagarin ejected from his capsule five kilometres above ground, landing by parachute near a very surprised six-year-old girl.

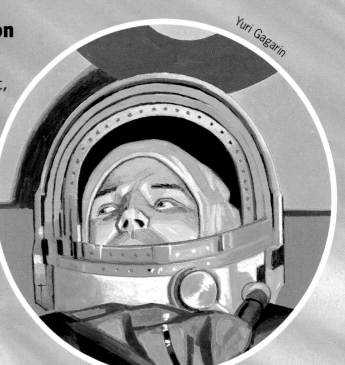

Yuri Gagarin

John Glenn's
Mercury capsule

## Who was the first American in space?

Alan Shepard just reached space on May 5, 1961. He stayed only a few seconds, but he inspired America to reach for the Moon. John Glenn was the first American to orbit the Earth.

**Amazing!** You can see the Great Wall of China from space. Especially at sunset and sunrise, the wall casts a very sharp shadow across the Chinese landscape, and is quite visible to the naked eye. Without the help of a telescope, you can also make out city lights, and even supertankers!

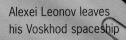
Alexei Leonov leaves
his Voskhod spaceship

## ? Who made the first space walk?

Alexei Leonov walked in space on March 18, 1965. He was roped to his space capsule to stop him floating away. His spacesuit ballooned with air, and he had to let most of it out before he could fit back inside the capsule!

### Is it true?
*Sally Ride was the first woman in space.*

**NO.** Valentina Tereshkova, a Soviet Russian textile worker, retrained as a pilot. She blasted into space on June 16, 1963, staying up in Vostok 6 for nearly three days. Later that year, she married another Soviet space traveller, Andrian Nikolayev. Sally Ride was the first American woman to reach space, on the space shuttle Challenger, in 1983.

Valentina Tereshkova

129

## Who was the first person on the Moon?

Neil Armstrong was the first man to step on to the surface of the Moon, on Sunday, July 20, 1969. Armstrong called it one small step for man, one giant leap for mankind. He was followed out by Buzz Aldrin, while Michael Collins orbited the Moon above them.

Neil Armstrong

## Is it true?

*Astronauts played golf on the Moon.*

**YES.** Apollo 14 arrived on the Moon in February, 1971, flown by Alan Shepard, America's first man in space, and Edgar Mitchell. They took rock samples and did some scientific experiments. After completing all their serious research work, Alan Shepard took out a golf club he had put together, and struck a few balls. They flew 370 metres in the low Moon gravity, much further than they would have done on Earth.

**Amazing!** There is no wind on the Moon, so flags need a wire along the top to hold them out straight. The first flag was planted by Armstrong and Aldrin. They put it so close to their lander that it was knocked over when they blasted off.

## Who took a car to the Moon?

The Apollo 15 crew took a Lunar Rover to the Moon in 1971. David Scott and James Irwin drove the battery-powered car around at speeds up to 11 kph. It had a satellite dish, a TV camera and baskets to carry moon rocks.

Lunar Rover

Apollo 13

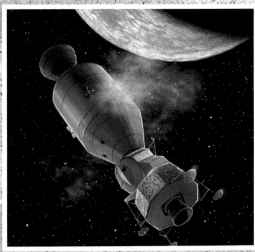

## For whom was the number 13 unlucky?

James Lovell and his crew were flying to the Moon in Apollo 13, on April 13, 1970, when vital oxygen tanks exploded, disabling the spacecraft. The Moon mission was cancelled. Ground Control worked very hard and managed to bring them home successfully.

## ❓ Which spacecraft is reusable?

The space shuttle was the world's first reusable spacecraft. Instead of a stack of rocket stages, it has separate booster rockets and a big fuel tank. The shuttle drops these before reaching orbit. It eventually glides back to Earth using its wings.

**3** Eventually the shuttle returns to Earth to be used again.

3

**2** The fuel tank is jettisoned and burns up in the atmosphere. This is the only part that isn't reused.

2

1

MMU in action

**1** The rocket boosters detach themselves and float back to Earth by parachute to be reused.

## ❓ What is an MMU?

The Manned Manoeuvring Unit, or MMU, is a small strap-on spacecraft. Together with a space suit, the MMU lets an astronaut move freely through space. It uses 24 tiny jets of gas to travel in any direction.

**Amazing!** The shuttle has a special area for cargo. It can hold up to 29 tonnes. That's the size and weight of an adult humpback whale!

## What does the space shuttle do?

The shuttle was first used for taking large satellites into orbit. After one shuttle blew up in 1986, NASA decided to use unmanned rockets again for launching satellites. The shuttle is now devoted to research, repairing satellites in orbit, and to building a space station.

Shuttle nose tiles

 **Is it true?**
*The shuttle is protected by tiles.*

**YES.** The shuttle is made from aluminium. This metal is very light, but it melts at high temperatures. A shuttle can heat up to 3,000°C as it returns to Earth, so it needs 20,000 heat proof tiles, which are glued on to its nose and belly.

Voyager probe passing Neptune

## Which voyagers visited all the planets?

Humans can't travel to other planets yet. A trip to Mars would need much bigger spacecraft than the shuttle. Instead, unmanned space probes like Voyager can travel through the solar system, sending home pictures of the planets.

### Is it true?
*A Mariner took photos of Mercury.*

**YES.** A very successful space probe called Mariner 10 visited the planet Mercury three times in the 1970s. As well as taking photos, Mariner discovered Mercury's strange magnetic field, and signs of ice at the poles.

## Which probe got too hot?

Four Venera probes have landed on Venus. The temperature there is a sweaty 460°C. As if that wasn't nasty enough, the clouds rain pure sulphuric acid!

Venera probe

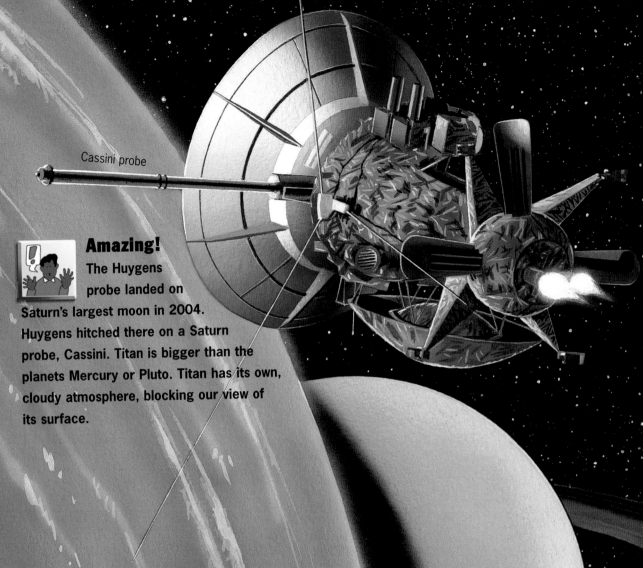

Cassini probe

## Amazing!

The Huygens probe landed on Saturn's largest moon in 2004. Huygens hitched there on a Saturn probe, Cassini. Titan is bigger than the planets Mercury or Pluto. Titan has its own, cloudy atmosphere, blocking our view of its surface.

## ? Which probe visited a comet?

Giotto was made to visit Halley's Comet as it passed Earth in 1986. Giotto had a special shield to protect it from the dust of the comet's tail. The probe took measurements and photographs from 600 km away, revealing the rocky heart of the comet.

Giotto passing Halley's Comet

## Is it true?

*There is life on Mars.*

**NO.** Probes have tested Martian soil for life. They added food to the soil to see if there was anything living there that was hungry! There wasn't. Then scientists found what looked like fossils inside a rock from Mars. After careful checking, they decided that the shapes were probably odd looking crystals. So there is no life on Mars, unless it is very good at hiding from us!

## What bounced around on Mars?

The Mars Pathfinder probe dropped on to Mars inside a bundle of balloons. The balloons bounced away from the falling parachute and deflated, then the Sojourner rover slowly drove away over them.

## Who drove a vehicle on Mars?

The Mars Pathfinder (1997) had a small, six-wheeled rover, called Sojourner. It used a camera and laser beams to find its way. Scientists on Earth asked Sojourner to examine particular objects, by radio. But the robot car had to decide how to reach them.

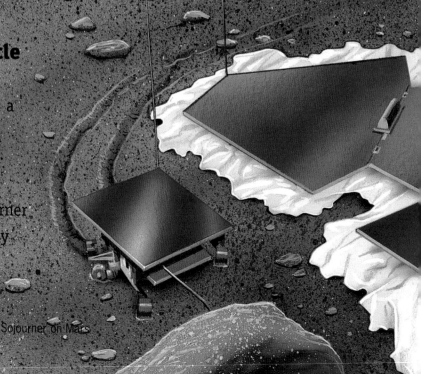

Sojourner on Mars

## ? Did Vikings really land on Mars?

Two space probes, called Viking 1 and Viking 2, landed on Mars in the 1970s. They took 3,000 photos, some in 3-D, and beamed them back to Earth. The Viking probes also measured weather patterns and examined the soil for signs of life. They didn't find any aliens.

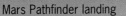
Mars Pathfinder landing

Mars probe

 **Amazing!** For 20 years before Pathfinder, several probes sent to Mars ended in disaster. A total of 16 probes from Russia either exploded on launch, missed the planet, or crashed into its surface. The American probe Observer exploded as it entered Mars's orbit. Some probes just went missing. Nobody knows why.

137

**Amazing!** John Glenn went to space at the age of 77. Sensors on his skin were used to monitor his health. His record-breaking flight happened 36 years after his first space trip, when he was the first American to orbit the Earth.

John Glenn

## Who is building a new space station?

America is leading a group of countries to build an international space station (ISS). The space shuttle is used to deliver parts. Most are made in America, but there are Japanese, Russian, Canadian and European parts as well. ISS uses giant solar panels to make its own electricity.

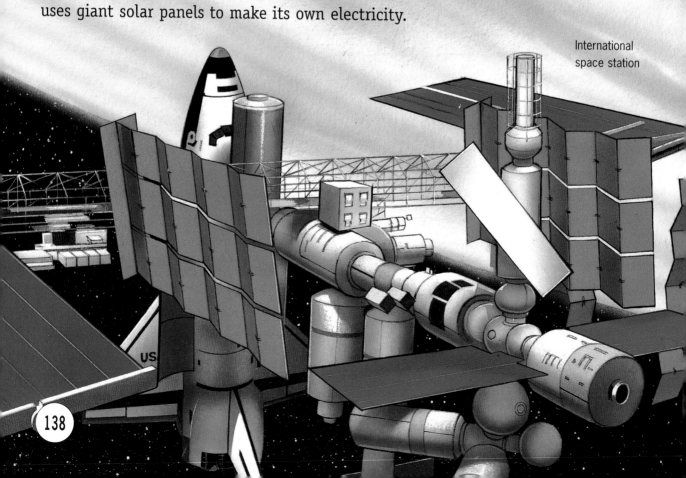

International space station

US

## Will there ever be a Moon base?

If space gets a lot busier it will make sense to use the Moon as a base. The Moon's low gravity lets big spacecraft take off and land easily compared to Earth.

Future Moon base

### Is it true?
*People can be 'buried' in space.*

**YES.** A cheap new rocket called Pegasus has made space funerals possible. The rocket delivered 25 people's ashes into space in 1997. For under £3,000 each, the ashes were scattered in orbit. They will drift back to Earth after a few years.

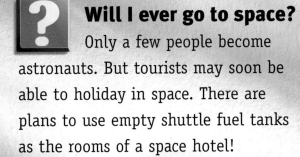

## Will I ever go to space?

Only a few people become astronauts. But tourists may soon be able to holiday in space. There are plans to use empty shuttle fuel tanks as the rooms of a space hotel!

Space hotel of the future

# Glossary

**Airship** A lighter-than-air aircraft with engines to make it move along.

**Amphibious** Capable of moving both on land and in the water.

**Articulated** A vehicle which is capable of bending in the middle.

**Axle** A straight rod at the base of a vehicle, which connects a pair of wheels.

**Biplane** A small aeroplane with two pairs of wings.

**Boosters** The parts of a rocket used to push a spacecraft into orbit.

**Bow** The front part of a ship. It is normally pointed to break easily through the water.

**Brakes** Devices that slow a vehicle. They work by pressing pads firmly against the spinning wheels.

**Chassis** The central base of a vehicle, on to which the axles and bodywork are attached.

**Clutch** A device on a vehicle, which controls whether or not the power from an engine reaches the wheels.

**Comet** A ball of rock and ice which passes through the solar system, emitting long glowing tails, as it nears the sun.

**Convertible** A car with a fabric roof which folds down for open-air driving.

**Cylinder** A chamber inside an engine inside which pistons move up and down.

**Diesel engine** A type of internal combustion engine that uses diesel oil as fuel.

**Drag** A force caused by air flowing around a moving object which slows it down.

**Drive shaft** A rod that links an engine with the wheels of a vehicle. The engine turns the rod, which turns the wheels.

**Dug-out** A type of canoe made by hollowing out a large tree trunk.

**Exhaust pipes** Metal pipes which direct the waste gases from the engine into the air.

**Fuselage** The main part of a plane where passengers and crew sit and cargo is carried.

**Gears** Sets of cogs which transfer power from a vehicle's engine to its wheels. By selecting different gears, the driver can start off and travel at different speeds.

**Generator** A machine which converts movement into electricity.

**Glider** An aeroplane without an engine.

**Gravity** The force of attraction between objects, such as you and the Earth.

**Ground Control** A big team of experts on Earth who look after each space mission.

**Horsepower** A measurement of engine power equal to 745.7 watts. A family car produces around 150 horsepower per tonne.

**Hull** The main part of ship or boat. It keeps the boat watertight and supports the decks.

**Hydraulic** Worked by liquid. Liquid pumped to the cylinders moves pistons in or out to make a machine's parts move.

**Hydroplane** A light, flat-bottomed motorboat, which skims along the surface of the water, when driven at high speed.

**Internal combustion engine** A machine which converts the energy in fuel into movement by burning it with air inside cylinders.

**Jet engine** An engine which pushes an aircaft forwards by burning liquid fuel, and sending a jet of hot gas backwards.

**Knot** The measurement of speed at sea. One knot equals 1.85 kph.

**Laser** An intense beam of light which can be used to transfer energy across space.

**Liquid Oxygen** Oxygen is the gas in the air that allows things to burn. Rockets carry oxygen in liquid form to burn where there is no air.

**Mach** The measurement of the speed of sound – Mach 2 is twice the speed of sound.

**Magnets** Objects which attract or repel metal. In trains, very strong magnets are powered by electricity.

**Monoplane** An aeroplane with one pair of wings.

**Moon** Any large, roughly ball-shaped natural satellite orbiting a planet.

**Nuclear waste** Dangerous waste material from nuclear power plants.

**Petrol engine** An engine in which the pistons are pushed out by a mixture of petrol and air exploding.

**Pistons** Sliding parts inside an engine which push the wheels around.

**Planet** A large body orbiting a star, usually more than 1,000 kilometres wide.

**Pollution** The mess caused by fuel-burning machines, which can be dangerous.

**Propeller** A set of blades. When a ship's propeller spins round in the water, it pushes the ship along.

**Radar** A machine which sends radio waves into the sky and works out where objects are by detecting how the waves bounce back.

**Radiator** Part of the cooling system of a car. Air flowing past the radiator cools the hot water which has taken heat from the engine.

**Rechargeable** Describes a battery which can have its electricity replaced after it has run down. All cars have a rechargeable battery.

**Roll-cage** A strong metal frame which surrounds the driver of a roofless racing car. If a car flips upside down, the roll-cage makes the car roll over into an upright position.

**Rudder** A flap at the stern of a ship or boat that turns from side to side to make the ship or boat turn left or right.

**Space station** A huge satellite with living space for a crew of astronauts and scientists.

**Steam engine** A type of engine in which the pistons are moved inside cylinders by the pressure of steam created in a boiler.

**Stern** The back part of a ship.

**Suspension** The series of springs

and dampers on the underside of a vehicle. The suspension allows the vehicle to travel comfortably over bumps on the road.

**Throttle** The device on a car or motorbike, also known as the accelerator, which controls the flow of fuel to the engine.

**Tractor unit** The front section of an articulated truck, where the cab and engine are located.

**Trailer** The rear section of an articulated truck, where the cargo is carried.

**Trams** Electric trains which run in city streets, cleaner and quieter than buses.

**Tread** The pattern of grooves around the outside of a tyre.

**Triplane** An aeroplane with three sets of wings.

# Index